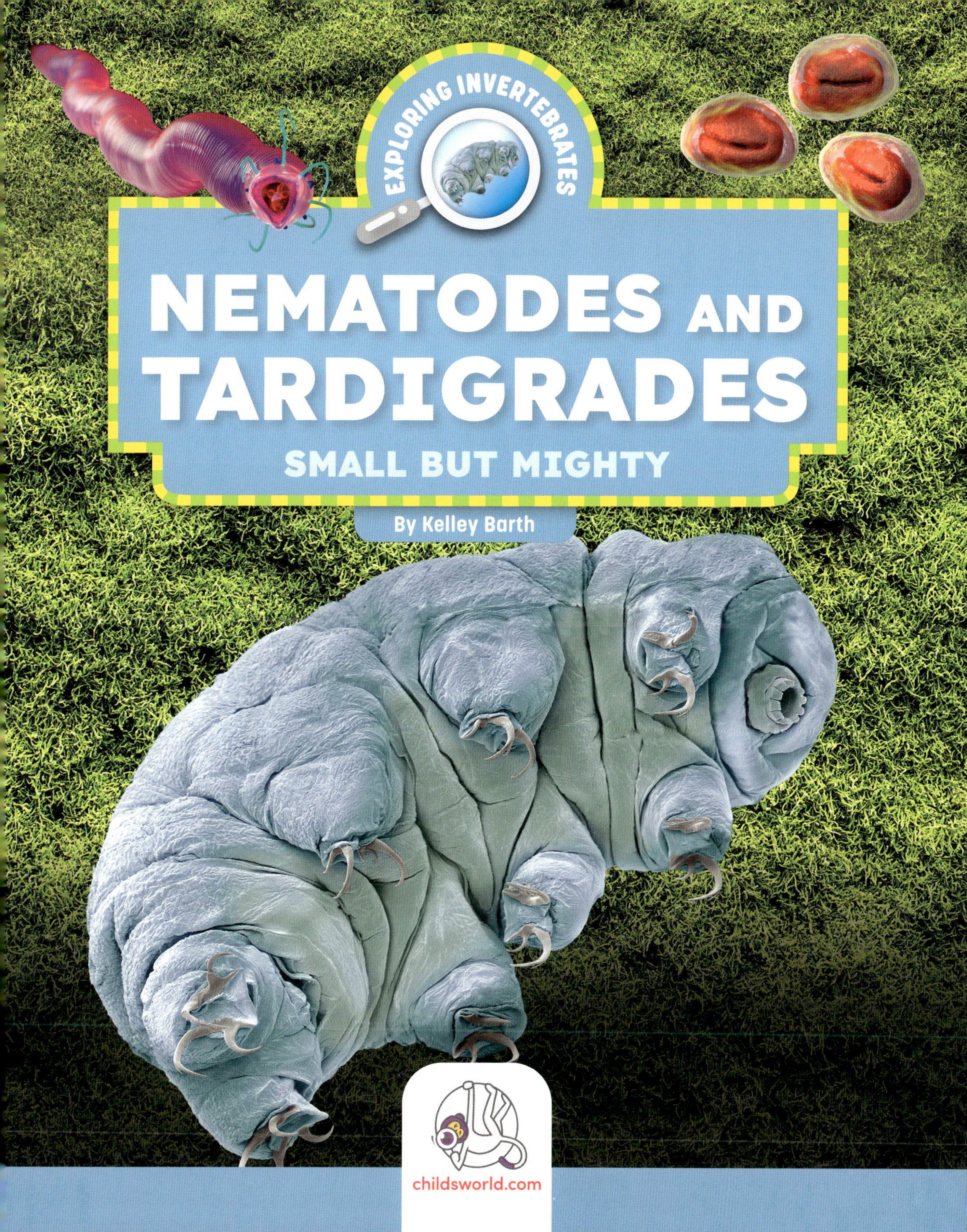
EXPLORING INVERTEBRATES
NEMATODES AND TARDIGRADES
SMALL BUT MIGHTY
By Kelley Barth
childsworld.com

Published by The Child's World®
800-599-READ • childsworld.com

Photography Credits
Cover: ©Steve Gschmeissner/Science Photo Library/Getty Images; ©Science Artwork/Science Photo Library/Getty Images; ©Katerina Kon/Science Photo Library/Getty Images; page 5: ©Sinhyu/Getty Images; ©chanisara.P/Shutterstock; page 6: ©ALEAIMAGE/Getty Images; page 7: ©koosen/Shutterstock; ©Roland Birke/Getty Images; ©Ed Reschke/Getty Images; ©New Africa/Shutterstock; page 9: ©Servier Medical Art/flickr; ©Pepermpron/Shutterstock; ©Eveleen/Shutterstock; page 10: ©Science Artwork/Science Photo Library/Getty Images; page 11: ©Steve Gschmeissner/Science Photo Library/Getty Images; page 12: ©Robert Pickett/Getty Images; ©Steve Gschmeissner/Science Photo Library/Getty Images; page 13: ©Shin Okamoto/Getty Images; page 14: ©picture alliance/Getty Images; page 15: ©PubMed/researchgate.net; page 17: ©Lam Van Linh/Shutterstock; ©page 19: ©Astrid860/Getty Images; page 22: ©anat chant/Shutterstock

ISBN Information
9781503894549 (Reinforced Library Binding)
9781503894785 (Portable Document Format)
9781503895607 (Online Multi-user eBook)
9781503896420 (Electronic Publication)

LCCN
2024942890

Printed in the United States of America

ABOUT THE AUTHOR

Kelley Barth is a former children's librarian who loves connecting with young people over stories and books. When she isn't busy writing, she enjoys reading, hiking, crafting, and going on adventures with her husband and son.

CONTENTS

MEET THE SMALL BUT MIGHTY

A scientist places a drop of water on a small piece of glass. At first, it looks like an ordinary droplet of water. But then the scientist slides the glass underneath a microscope. She adjusts the focus and zooms in on the droplet. Suddenly, there is a lot to see! There are many animals living inside of that tiny droplet. These animals are **microscopic**. You can't see them with just your eyes. But with the microscope, the scientist can observe them in hopes of learning more. These animals may be small. But their impact on our world is huge.

Roundworms are nematodes that can cause illnesses in humans, dogs, cats, and many other animals.

Many nematodes can only be seen through a powerful microscope.

THE LIFE OF A NEMATODE

Nematodes (NEH-muh-tohdz) are a type of small **invertebrate**. A nematode's body is shaped like a tube. They have a mouth at one end where they eat food. Waste exits from the other end of the tube. Most nematodes are see-through. They are covered by a tough, flexible covering called a **cuticle**. Nematodes often **molt** their cuticle as they grow. Some nematodes are called roundworms or threadworms. They look a bit like earthworms you might see in dirt. But their bodies are smooth, and they are usually very small.

NEMATODE SIZE COMPARISON*

Many nematodes are microscopic. They are smaller than the tip of a pencil. Others can grow very long. The longest nematode can grow up to 27.6 feet (8.4 meters) long. That's almost the length of 44 pencils!

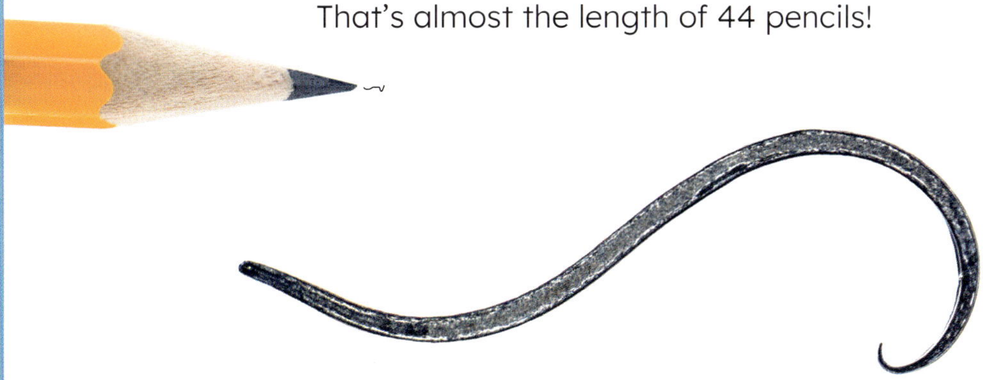

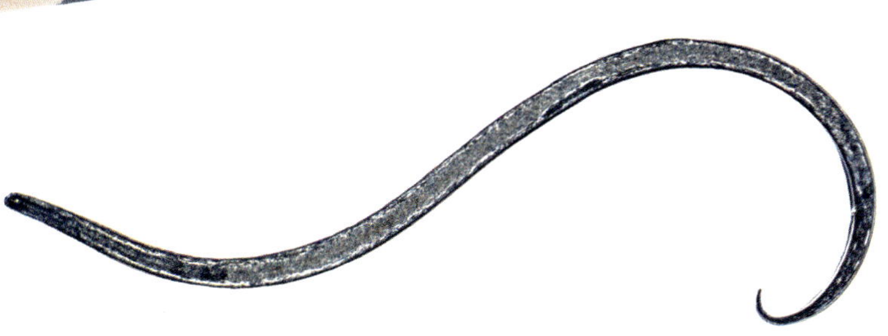

*images are not actual sizes

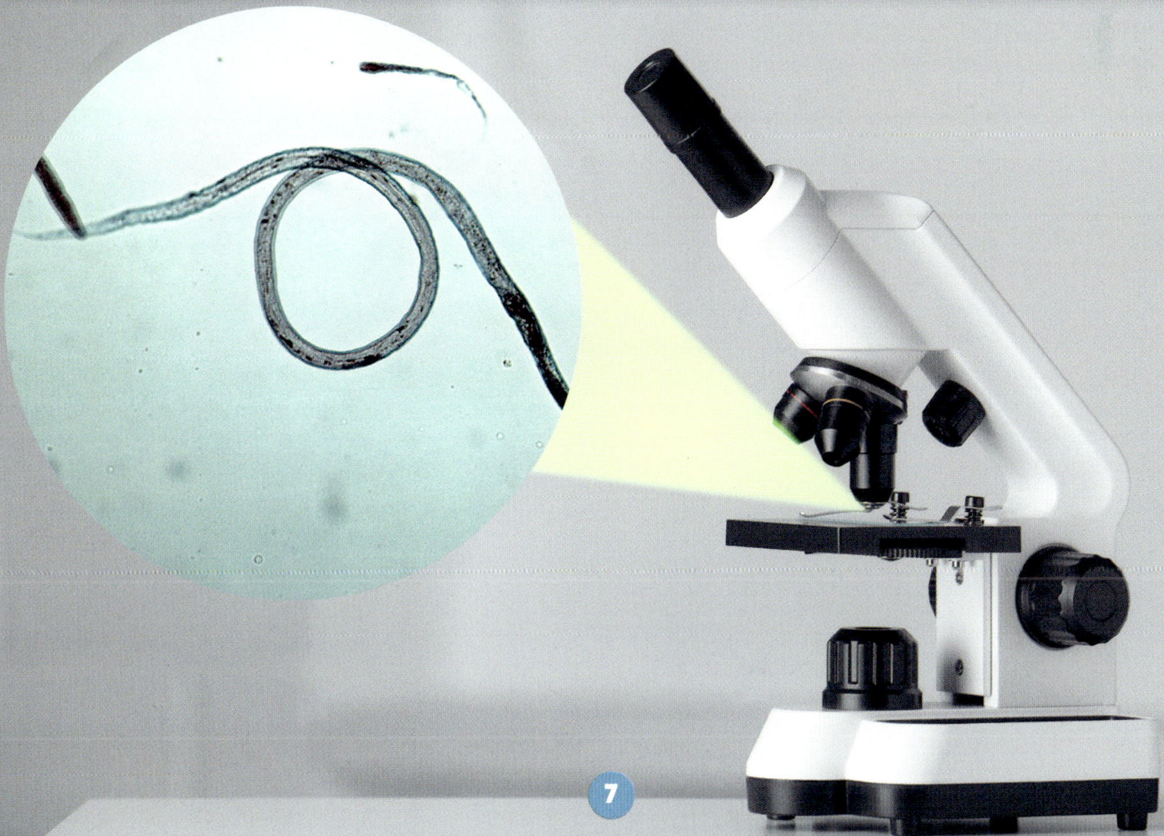

SO MANY NEMATODES!

You may not always see them, but nematodes are everywhere. In fact, around 80 percent of the world's animals are nematodes. One reason there are so many nematodes is that they have a lot of babies. Some nematodes can lay up to 200,000 eggs per day!

Nematodes are some of the most common animals on Earth. They live in many different places. Many live in soil. Thousands of nematodes can live in a single handful of dirt. Other nematodes live in salt water or fresh water. Nematodes can live almost anywhere, from polar icebergs to deep cracks in the bottom of the ocean.

Some nematodes don't live on their own. They are **parasites**. Parasites must live on a **host** to survive. Hosts can be plants or other animals. Some nematodes live inside human hosts. These parasites can make people sick.

LIFE CYCLE OF A HOOKWORM

Hookworms are parasites. They go through many life stages in their hosts.

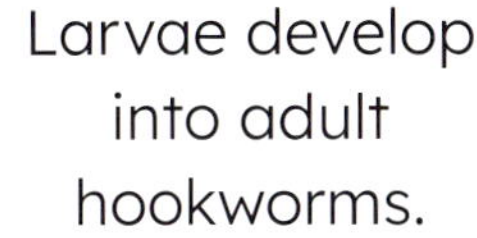

Larvae develop into adult hookworms.

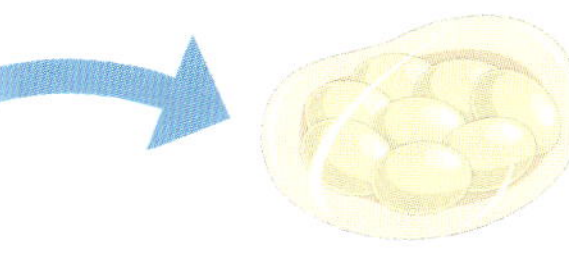

Eggs of a hookworm pass out of the body in the waste of a host.

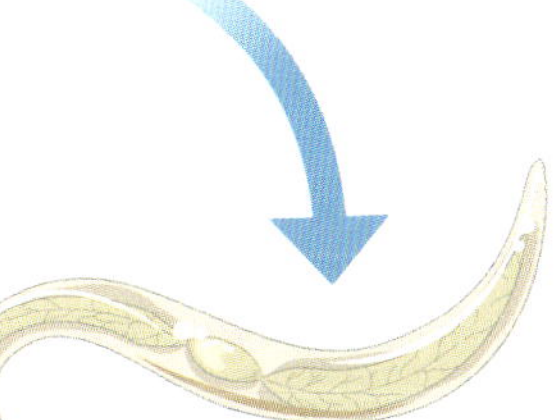

Eggs develop into **larvae**.

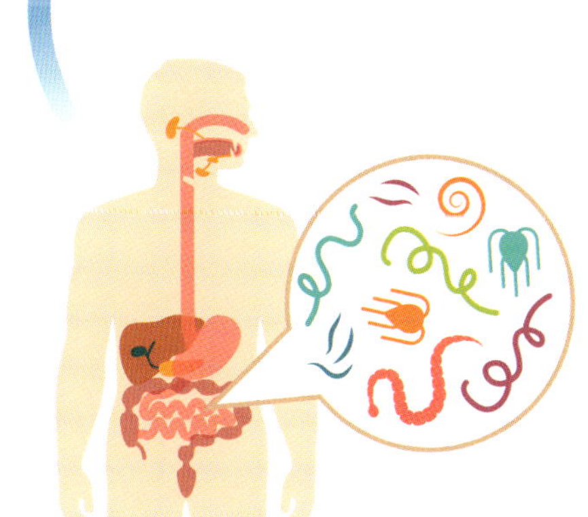

Larvae move through the host's body into the intestine.

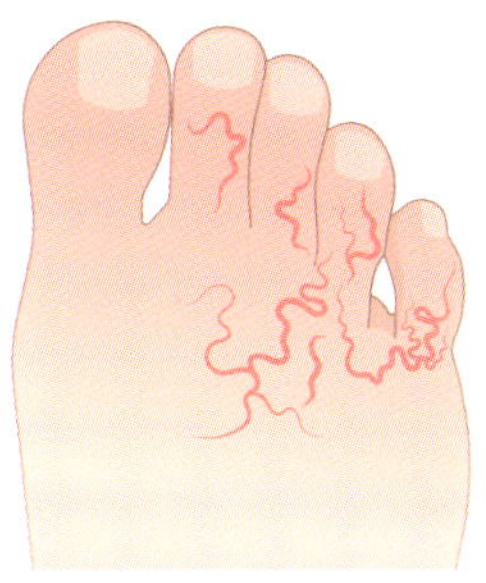

Larvae enter a new host.

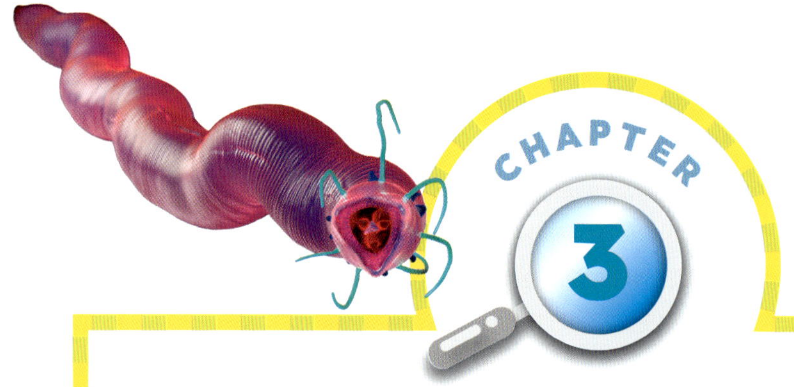

THE LIFE OF A TARDIGRADE

Tardigrades (TAR-duh-graydz) are also small-but-mighty animals. They are smaller than a single grain of sand. Tardigrade bodies are split into four parts, or **segments**. Each segment has two short legs. Each of the legs has sharp claws, like a bear. Tardigrade heads have short snouts and sharp teeth, like a pig. They are sometimes called water bears or moss piglets.

Like nematodes, tardigrades lay eggs. They also molt throughout their life as they grow larger. Tardigrades eat **bacteria** and juices from plants such as algae or moss. Some even eat other tardigrades.

LET'S TAKE A LOOK!

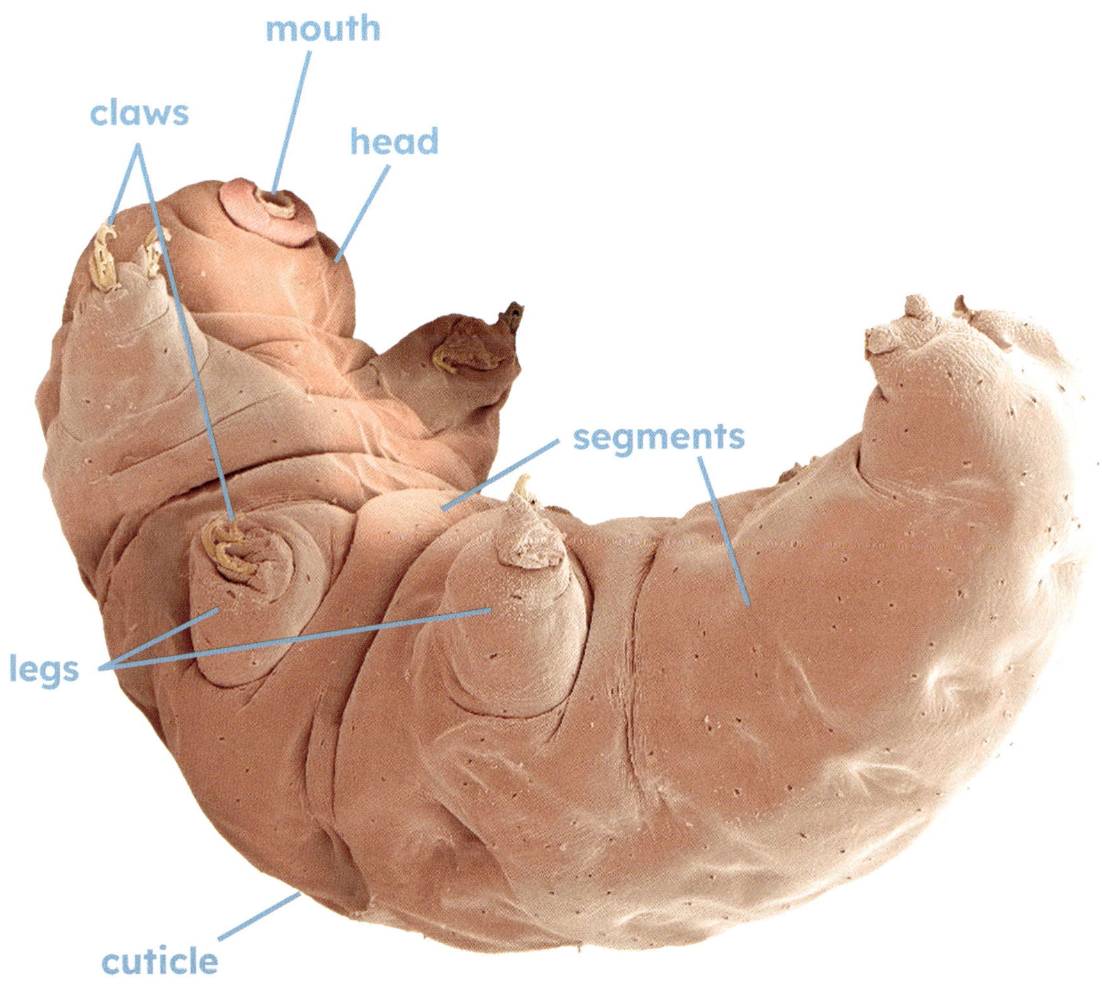

mouth

claws

head

segments

legs

cuticle

Tardigrades are only visible with a microscope.
When an image of a tardigrade is captured with a microscope, scientists use computer technology to create a realistic-looking image of the creature.

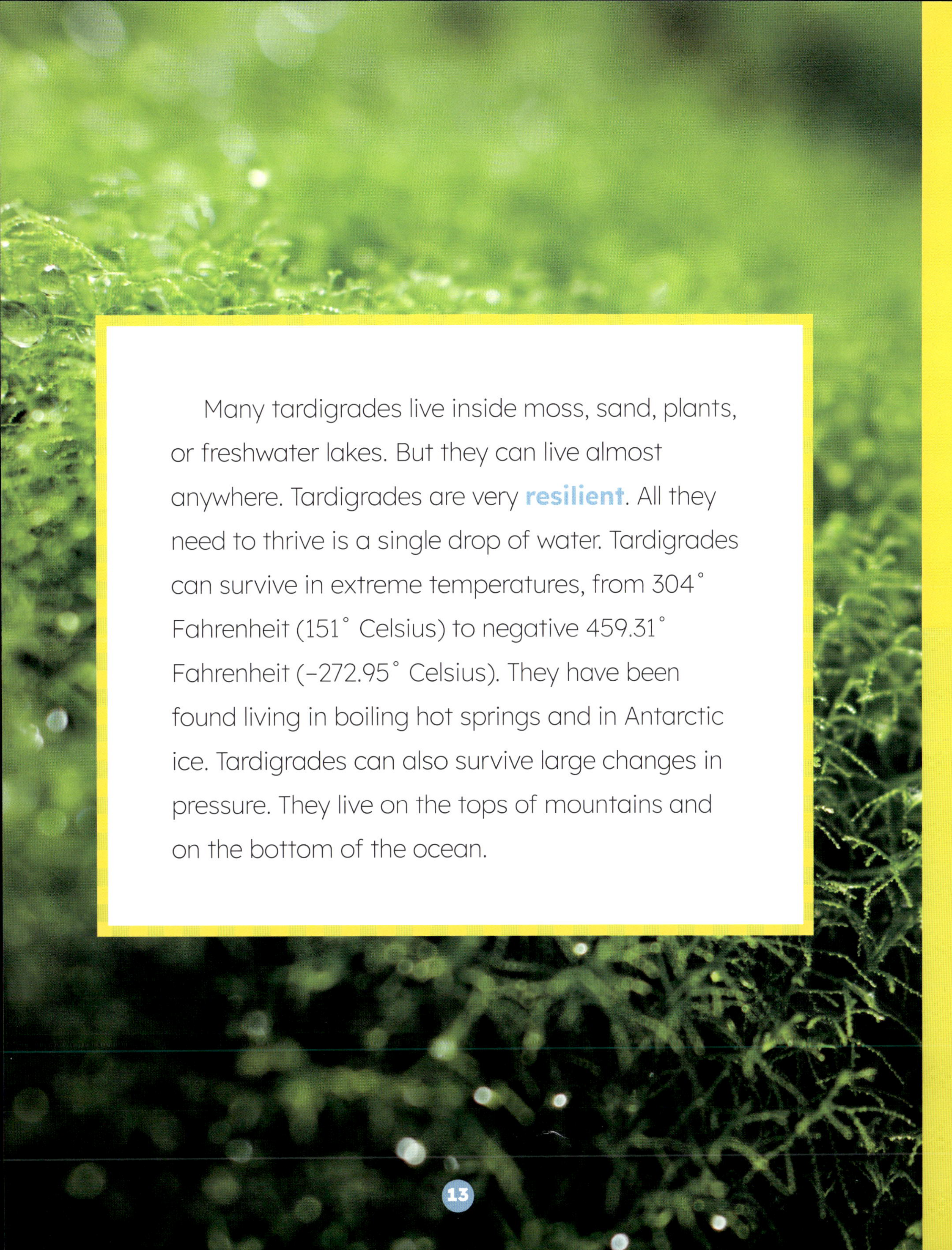

Many tardigrades live inside moss, sand, plants, or freshwater lakes. But they can live almost anywhere. Tardigrades are very **resilient**. All they need to thrive is a single drop of water. Tardigrades can survive in extreme temperatures, from 304° Fahrenheit (151° Celsius) to negative 459.31° Fahrenheit (−272.95° Celsius). They have been found living in boiling hot springs and in Antarctic ice. Tardigrades can also survive large changes in pressure. They live on the tops of mountains and on the bottom of the ocean.

TARDIGRADES IN SPACE

Tardigrades haven't just survived in extreme places on Earth. They have also traveled to outer space! Scientists wanted to see if tardigrades were able to survive in space. In 2007, a group of tardigrades spent 10 days floating in space. Many of the animals survived the freezing temperatures and lack of air. Some even were able to survive the strong **radiation** blasts.

By enlarging a tardigrade to 1,000 times its normal size, scientists can learn more about the creature's organs and how it's able to survive such harsh conditions.

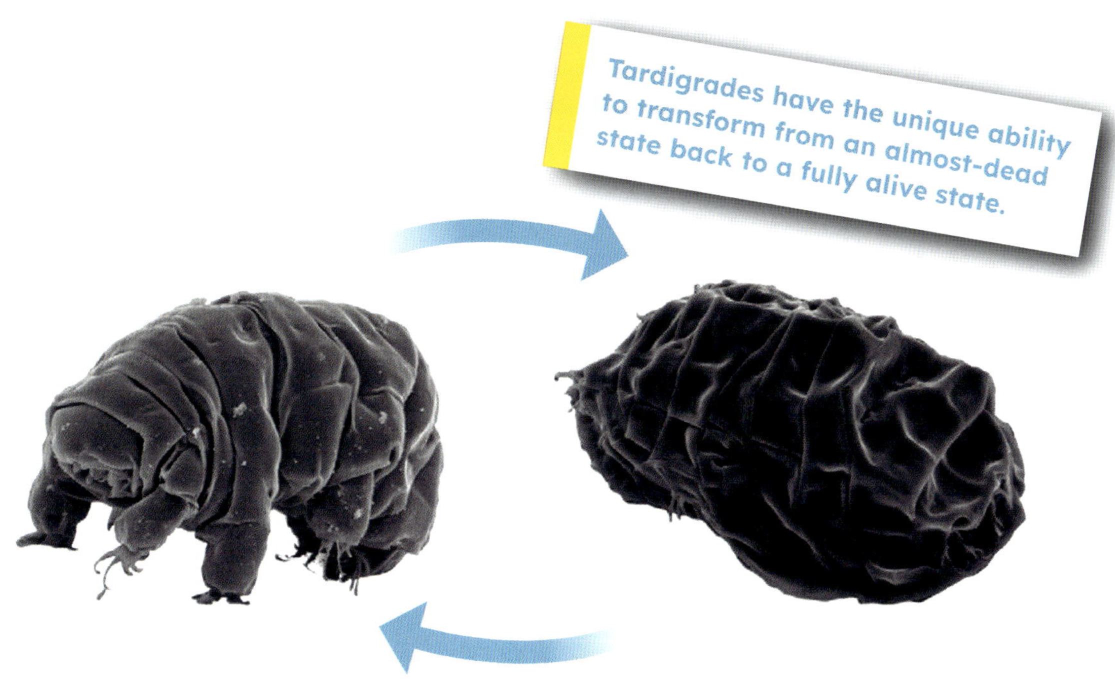

Tardigrades have developed a special ability to survive extreme conditions. They can even survive without water or oxygen. Without water, tardigrades curl up into a small, dry ball. This is called a **tun**. As a tun, their body systems slow down. Tardigrades may look dead. But they are still alive. They are in a very deep, long-lasting sleep. When a tun is exposed to water, the tardigrade can fully come back to life in a few hours. Tardigrades can survive as a tun for more than 30 years!

THE SMALL BUT MIGHTY WORLD

Even small animals can cause big problems. Nematodes cause a lot of destruction and disease. Some nematodes that live in soil can harm the plants around them. Nematodes often eat plant roots and harm food crops.

Parasitic nematodes are also a big health problem. Over one billion people have a nematode parasite. Pets and farm animals can also get diseases from nematodes. The best way to prevent a nematode infection is to practice good hygiene. Wash your hands often and make sure to clean and cook your food well.

Nematodes are often the cause of crop issues for farmers. Thousands of tiny nematodes can be found in a small patch of soil.

But these tiny creatures don't just cause problems. Most nematodes help the environment. They are known as **decomposers**. Decomposers break down dead plants. This helps keep soil healthy and allows new plants to grow. Many nematodes eat pests that eat plants. Some farmers use them to help protect crops.

Tardigrades play another important role in the environment, too. They are a **pioneer species**. Pioneer species are the first things to live in a new environment. They help make the environment healthy so more plants and animals can live there. Many animals also eat nematodes and tardigrades. They are important parts of the food chain.

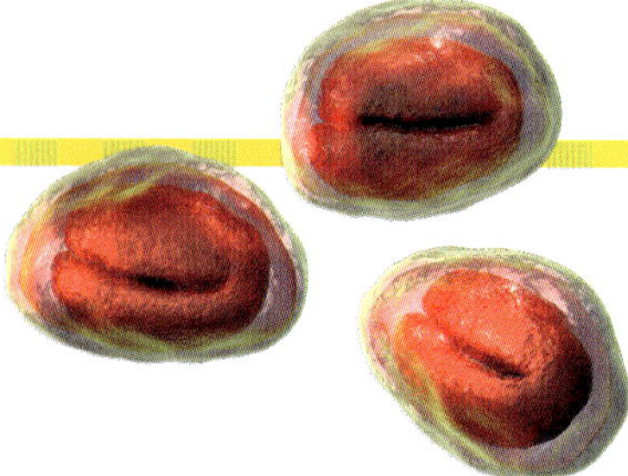

Not all nematodes cause problems for plants. Some feed on decaying matter and help the soil stay healthy.

CHAPTER 5

THE FUTURE OF NEMATODES AND TARDIGRADES

Nematodes and tardigrades have been around since before the dinosaurs. But there is still so much we don't know about them. Scientists are always learning more about these small-but-mighty animals.

Some nematodes make people sick, but scientists think some might be able to help cure diseases. Scientists are also studying tardigrades. Understanding how tardigrades survive in extreme environments might help humans do the same in the future. These animals might be small, but there is still a lot we have to learn from them.

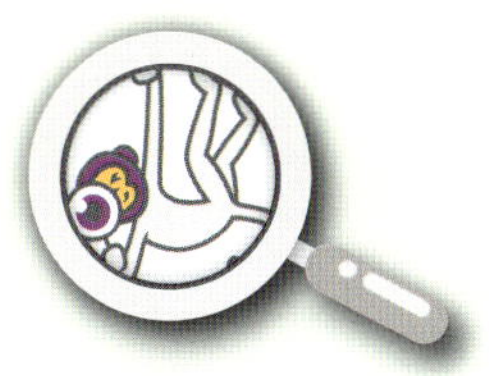

WONDER MORE

Wondering About New Information

What did you learn about nematodes and tardigrades? Write down three new facts you learned. Did this information surprise you? Why or why not?

Wondering How It Matters

You have probably never seen a nematode or tardigrade, but they are living all around you. What are some other things that are small but mighty? How do they impact the world even though they are small?

Wondering Why

Tardigrades and nematodes are known for being able to survive in many different environments. What are some other animals that are able to live in extreme environments? How do they manage to survive?

Ways to Keep Wondering

After reading this book, what questions do you have about nematodes and tardigrades? What can you do to learn more about them?

FINDING TARDIGRADES

Tardigrades may be able to survive in extreme environments, but many live right in your own neighborhood. Search your environment to see if you can find some tardigrades.

Steps to Take

1. Collect a small clump of moss. This is a popular place for tardigrades to live.
2. Soak the moss in water (rainwater is best) for a few hours.
3. Squeeze the water out of the moss and collect it in a shallow, glass dish.
4. Examine the collected water under a microscope. Do you see any tardigrades? If not, try another moss clump from a different location. What are you able to observe?

Supplies

- microscope
- shallow, glass dish (petri dish if possible)
- moss

GLOSSARY

bacteria (back-TEER-ee-uh) Bacteria are microscopic living things that can be found in all natural environments.

cuticle (KYOO-ti-kul) A cuticle is a hard or waxy outer covering of an invertebrate.

decomposers (dee-kuhm-POH-zerz) Decomposers are animals that eat and break down dead plant or animal matter.

host (HOST) A host is a living plant or animal that a parasite lives in or on.

invertebrate (in-VUR-tuh-bruht) Invertebrates are animals that do not have a spine.

larvae (LAHR-vee) Larvae are animals after they hatch from eggs and before they become adults.

microscopic (my-kroh-SKAH-pik) Microscopic animals are very small and can only be seen through a microscope.

molt (MOHLT) Animals molt when they shed their outer skin in order to grow larger.

parasites (PAYR-uh-sites) Parasites are animals that live in or on another living thing, called a host.

pioneer species (py-uh-NEER SPEE-sheez) Pioneer species are the first plants and animals to live in a new environment.

radiation (ray-dee-AY-shun) Radiation is the energy that moves from one place to another.

resilient (ruh-ZIL-yent) Resilient animals are able to recover or adjust to change.

segments (SEG-muhnts) Segments are the parts into which a thing is divided.

tun (TUN) A tun is the state when a tardigrade turns into a small, dry ball without water.

FIND OUT MORE

In the Library

Jenkins, Steve and Robin Page. *Tiny Monsters: The Strange Creatures That Live On Us, In Us, and Around Us.* New York, NY: Houghton Mifflin Harcourt, 2020.

Lundgren, Julie, K. *Gross and Disgusting Parasites.* New York, NY: Crabtree Publishing Company, 2022.

Stone, Tiffany. *Super Small: Miniature Marvels of the Natural World.* Vancouver, Canada: Greystone Kids, 2023.

On the Web

Visit our website for links about nematodes and tardigrades:
childsworld.com/links

Note to Parents, Caregivers, Teachers, and Librarians: We routinely verify our web links to make sure they are safe and active sites. So encourage your readers to check them out!

INDEX